Published 2011
by

www.gotothehub.com

3405 Milton Avenue, Suite 207
Dallas, TX 75205

Printed in the United States

BIBLE STUDIES

BUY.RENT.DOWNLOAD

ECCLESIASTES

A Life Well Lived (A Study Of Ecclesiastes)
Bible Study Series by Tommy Nelson
  4 DVD Curriculum
  Companion Study Guide
  A Life Well Lived paperback book

PHILIPPIANS

Philippians, To Live Is Christ & To Die Is Gain
Bible Study Series by Matt Chandler
  4 DVD Curriculum
  Companion Study Guide
  Packages and bulk discounts available

ROMANS

Romans, The Letter That Changed The World, Vol. I & II
Bible Study Series by Tommy Nelson
  DVD Curriculum
  Companion Study Guide
  Packages and bulk discounts available

RUTH

NEW! *Ruth; Your God, My God. A True Story Of Love & Redemption*
Bible Study Series by Tommy Nelson
  4 DVD Curriculum
  Companion Study Guide
  Packages and bulk discounts available

SONG OF SOLOMON

Improved! *1995 Song Of Solomon Classic*
DVD Curriculum by Tommy Nelson
  Enhanced video, audio and color graphics
  Updated and enlarged companion Study Guide
  Formatted for Widescreen

Enhanced! *SOS For Students*
DVD Curriculum by Tommy Nelson
  Re-Mastered Video & Audio
  All new graphics and menus
  Never before seen Q & A's
  All in one Study Guide for both Students & Leaders

VINTAGE JESUS

Vintage Jesus, Timeless Answers To Timely Questions
Bible Study Series by Mark Driscoll
  4 DVD Curriculum
  Companion Study Guide
  Packages and bulk discounts available

ACKNOWLEDGEMENTS

The Hub wishes to thank the following friends without whose help this series and study guide would not have been possible:

Jim Gribnitz, Crosswise Media (Study Guide Consultant) • **Shatrine Krake**, Krake Designs • **Sandy Orellana** • **Jason Countryman**, PocketPak Albums

All of our sponsors: without their commitment to Pastor Mark Driscoll, this message and this tour would not be possible. So, thank you to: Logos Bible Software, Food for the Hungry, The Resurgence, Vryso, Bible Study Magazine, and 5 Love Languages.

Mars Hill Church and their entire team: who God has and is raising up to be another truly unique and powerful voice for the Gospel. We want to thank the team at pastormark.tv for their creative and tireless effort to support this message and tour. And, much thanks to Thomas Nelson Publishers who saw the vision and helped create and build the resources for the *Real Marriage* book and curriculum series, and thanks for the partnership to support Pastor Mark and Grace in their book.

ABOUT THE HUB

Thanks for taking a moment to learn more about us. Our organization began in 1995 working with one speaker, Tommy Nelson and one amazing message, The Song of Solomon. It was and is our privilege to help champion God's written Word on Love, Dating, Marriage and Sex based directly on Song of Solomon. It is a book that has been censored for centuries and it has been a total blessing and thrill to see it change my life, and millions of others.

As of August 2009 we have re-branded our organization to reflect the root of our passion and the future of our organization:

To Develop, Find and Share life changing Bible-Centric tools that move people forward. We have renamed our organization to The Hub. It is our passion and commitment to be a Hub for unique, challenging, and grace-filled resources. I hope you will agree after you participate and interact with one of our resources. God Bless you and know that if you will listen, God's Truth will move you forward in life, no matter where you have been or are currently.

Doug Hudson, President - The Hub

TABLE OF CONTENTS

ᴛʜᴇ DRISCOLLS' BIOGRAPHY

Pastor MARK DRISCOLL is the founding pastor of Mars Hill Church in Seattle, Washington and is one of the world's most-downloaded and quoted pastors. His audience—fans and critics alike—spans the theological and cultural left and right. He was also named one of the "25 Most Influential Pastors of the Past 25 Years" by *Preaching* magazine, and his sermons are consistently #1 on iTunes each week for Religion & Spirituality with over 10 million downloads each year.

Pastor Mark received a B.A. in Speech Communication from the Edward R. Murrow School of Communication at Washington State University, and he holds a masters degree in Exegetical Theology from Western Seminary in Portland, Oregon. He is the author of fifteen books.

GRACE DRISCOLL delights in being a stay at home mom and helping raise the Driscolls' three sons and two daughters. She is also a graduate of the Edward R. Murrow School of Communication at Washington State University, where she earned a B.A. in Public Relations.

In 1996, at the age of twenty-five, Pastor Mark and his wife Grace, acted on their vision to make disciples of Jesus and plant churches. They started a small Bible study at their home in Seattle, which at the time was the least churched city in America. Since that time, by God's grace, the church has exploded with upwards of nineteen thousand people meeting across thirteen locations in four states (Washington, Oregon, California, and New Mexico). Mars Hill has been recognized as the 54th largest, 30th fastest-growing, and 2nd most-innovative church in America by *Outreach* magazine.

Pastor Mark is the co-founder of the Acts 29 Network, which has planted over 400 churches in the US, in addition to thirteen other nations. He founded the Resurgence, which receives close to six million visits annually and services Christian leaders through books, blogs, conferences, and classes. He along with Pastor James McDonald co-founded Churches Helping Churches, which raised over $2.7 million to help rebuild churches in Haiti, and empower them to minister and provide aide to the Haitian community, as well as deliver $1.7 million in medical supplies to the devastated country.

With a skillful mix of bold presentation, clear biblical teaching, and compassion for those who are hurting the most—in particular, women who are victims of sexual and physical abuse and assault—Driscoll has taken biblical Christianity into cultural corners previously unexplored by evangelicals. In addition to speaking at a Gospel Coalition conference with notable contemporary theologians like John Piper and Tim Keller, he also discussed biblical sexuality as a guest on *Loveline with Dr. Drew*, was featured on *Nightline*, and preached for Rick Warren at Saddleback Community Church.

For anything and everything related to Pastor Mark & Grace Driscoll visit **www.pastormark.tv**.

Feel free to connect on Twitter and facebook as well:
www.twitter.com/pastormark
http://www.facebook.com/pastormark

PREFACE

How is your love life?

Are you single, hoping to meet someone and live happily ever after? Seeing someone and contemplating marriage? Maybe you're newly married and still filled with wedded bliss, or a married couple so exhausted from the constant demands of work and parenting that your marriage is slipping. You may be reeling from a devastating sin in your marriage. Or the two of you are still in love and doing pretty well, but you want to avoid ending up like other couples you know who are not getting along and possibly even getting divorced. Perhaps you are empty-nesters who have realized that your kids largely held your family together and you don't have a close friendship now that they're out of the house. Are you a parent or grandparent concerned for the marriage of your child or grandchild? Divorced and trying to figure out what went wrong and how not to endure that pain again? A leader who seeks to help people struggling with relationship issues?

Whether you or someone you know has a problem in marriage—or are trying to avoid one—my wife, Grace, and I hope to help.

We want to serve you in our book *Real Marriage*, on this tour, and in this study guide. So we will be honest about our own failures, sins, mistakes, and griefs. Even a pastor and his wife come into marriage with baggage and a few carry-ons.

But God has been faithful to us, and we trust Him to be faithful to you as well.

HOPE *for* SINGLES

Boaz took Ruth and she became his wife.
Ruth 4:13

BIG IDEA!

Single people run the gamut of emotions and contentment. Some are completely discontent and are primed to settle for the first warm body that jumps in their path, while some on the other extreme have an arrogance about their singleness and look down on others who are married in an effort to feel better about themselves. Both of these extremes are unhealthy.

My telling you, 'Land in the middle of these two extremes' is also believably unhelpful. Positing the two extremes and telling you to not be either of them leaves way too big of a middle range that becomes unhelpful in day-to-day living. Sort of like telling you, one coast has New York, and one has Seattle – meet me in the middle. Where exactly?

It is important to get practical as we press into this idea of singleness and not just look at actions that God would have us take, but talk about the way we ought to think about singleness as well.

It pains Grace and me to know that some of the biggest life decisions are made during this phase of life, and yet so little is done to speak practically and helpfully for you.

The pre-marriage phase is just as important as the marriage phase.

Here's why.

A LITTLE
BACKGROUND

Ruth is one of the most wonderfully written stories in all of Scripture. It is one of only two books in the entire Bible named after a woman (the other one being Esther), and the only one named after someone who was not racially Jewish. It focuses on a female friendship between the young, new convert Ruth and the older, bitter Naomi, and it centers on the lives of two older singles.

While there is uncertainty surrounding both the author (possibly Samuel) and date of authorship (possibly 1000 BC), there is no debate about who the hero of the story is. Throughout the book God works not through His visible hand of miracle, but more subtly through His invisible hand of providence. This point is emphasized throughout the story as God is mentioned 23 times, and 21 of those occurrences are by the characters in the story acknowledging how God is working through the people and circumstances of their life to bring about His purposes. As a result the book moves from death to life, barrenness to fruitfulness, cursing to blessing, bitterness to worship, and loneliness to community. In this the love, mercy, and kindness of God shines forth in an otherwise tragic tale.

The story opens in one of the darkest seasons of Old Testament history when God's people were living in sin during a famine. Naomi was a Jewish woman whose husband moved her to the godless country of Moab that was descended from incest in the days of Genesis. There, Naomi saw her sons marry Moabite

MOAB

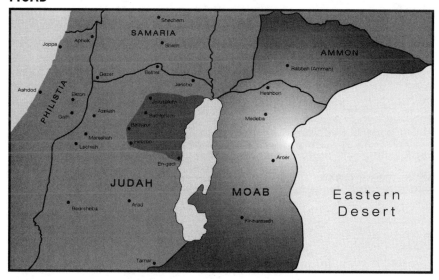

women and experienced the death of her sons and husband in Moab leaving her destitute and alone. Although admittedly bitter against God, Naomi decides to leave Moab and return home to God's people. One of her daughter-in-laws, Orpah, returned to her people and religion in Moab at Naomi's urging, but Naomi's other daughter-in-law, Ruth, was determined to leave her people and religion to worship Naomi's God and live with God's people.

Ruth and Naomi then make the roughly fifty mile journey from Moab to Bethlehem, a place pregnant with meaning as it is where Jesus was later to be born as promised in Micah 5:2. There, Ruth spends her time at the equivalent of the food bank trying to get enough food to keep her and Naomi alive. To make matters worse, as a Moabite she was likely to face intense racism and as a non-virgin likely to be mistreated and abused by men. Nonetheless, she shines forth as one of the godliest and most loyal, humble, and exemplary women in all of human history.

God providentially protects and provides for the women until He then brings into their life a godly man named Boaz who repeatedly cares for both Ruth and Naomi as the means by which God extended them His grace. Boaz is presented as an incredibly godly man who is spoken of in glowing terms by everyone in the book, from his employees to the women. Boaz is a godly, wealthy, and successful man who falls in love with Ruth after investigating her relationship with God and character until he is certain that she is the woman of his dreams. After Ruth gets all dressed up and puts herself in Boaz's way as Naomi instructed her, Boaz redeems Ruth, marries her, and cares for her and her mother-in-law. He is a type of Jesus, who redeems these women and blesses them in every way, treating the poor, widows, outcast, marginalized, and racially despised with redeeming love.

RUTH'S FAMILY TREE

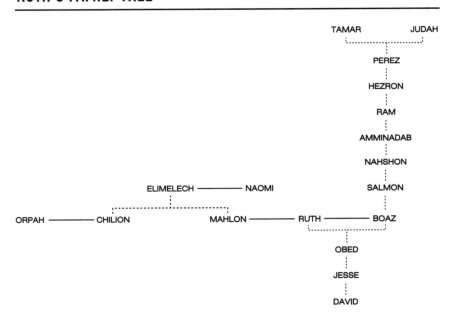

Throughout Ruth there are many prayers offered to God for a husband for Ruth (1:8-9), blessing for Boaz (2:12, 2:20), blessing for Ruth (3:10), and a child chosen by God for Kingdom purposes to be born for Ruth, Boaz, and Naomi to enjoy (4:11-12), and that God would be blessed and honored through the birth of their child (4:14). By the closing of the short book, every single prayer is answered by God.

> Selfishness is often mastered during singleness (Real Marriage).

Ruth and Boaz have a love that rivals any love story in human history. And, God gives them a son named Obed. Obed becomes the grandfather of the great King David, through whom 2 Samuel 7:1-7 promised would come Jesus Christ. Ruth is again mentioned in only one place in the entire New Testament. In Matthew 1, the foreigner Ruth is one of a few women included in the genealogy of Christ. Indeed, the inclusion of each woman reinforces the truth that Jesus Christ saves us by pure grace and blesses even the worst of people from the worst of families, as Boaz did Ruth.

In conclusion, while God is the hero of the story, Naomi, Ruth, and Boaz are wonderful mentors from whom we can learn much. Although Naomi was bitter about her life, she wisely chose to run to God and His people for her healing. Although Ruth was a new convert with no guarantee of safety or welcome, she ran to God and His people in faith that somehow God would providentially take care of her while she lived a life of holiness. And Boaz stands above most other men in Scripture as an example for every man, particularly young men who aspire to prepare themselves to be godly business leaders, husbands, and fathers.

> A single woman should only marry a man she respects and trusts enough to follow (Real Marriage).

FROM THE LOVE STORY OF RUTH & BOAZ
WE LEARN THE FOLLOWING PRINCIPLES FOR SINGLES:

1. God loves, saves, and uses people from even the worst backgrounds and family histories.

2. Even if you come from a godless home, you can have a godly marriage.

3. Older divorced and widowed people can still find godly spouses and love by God's grace.

4. Tragedies can make the best opportunities.

5. It is wise when pursuing a relationship to seek counsel from godly, older believers.

6. Character is what counts, especially when you think no one is watching.

> Like many, we entered marriage with a load of habits, secrets, and preconceptions that could have killed our marriage (Real Marriage).

7. A man who wants to marry needs to make some money.

8. Sometimes the family of God is a stronger bond than even blood family.

9. Combat the singleness idols of dependence and independence.

10. Maximize your singleness for God *(see 1 Cor. 7)*.

11. Be "the one" before you look for "the one".

12. If you love the Lord, only consider dating someone else who does too.

> Guys - keep your advice to a minimum and learn to listen. Resist the male urge to find a problem and try and fix it (Real Marriage).

13. Only be in a romantic relationship with one person at a time.

14. Practice chastity before marriage and fidelity in marriage.

15. God is at work in your love life. Don't overlook the people he puts in front of you.

16. It is okay for a woman to intentionally cross paths with a man she is interested in.

To learn more from the book of Ruth, my sermons in audio, video, and transcript formats are available for free at **http://marshill.com/media/redeemingruth**

WHAT NOW?

What are 1 to 2 practical things that you plan to do as a result of the teaching in this session?

1. _____

_____

_____

_____

2. _____

_____

_____

_____

your NOTES

FRIEND *with*
BENEFITS

2

This is my beloved,
and this is my friend. **Song of Songs 5:16**

BIG IDEA!

We read all or part of 187 books on marriage for research related to our book *Real Marriage*. Most of them were Christian books, and not one had any significant exploration of the subject of friendship within marriage. Indeed, we should study all the verses in the Bible related to marriage. But we should also study all the verses related to friendship because God intends for marriage to be between two friends.

In *Real Marriage* we say,
"*Husbands and wives who want their marriages to be enduring and endearing must be friends. One of the most respected sociologists studying marriage said, 'The determining factor in whether wives feel satisfied with the sex, romance, and passion in their marriage is, by 70 percent, the quality of the couple's friendship. For men, the determining factor is, by 70 percent, the quality of the couple's friendship. So men and women come from the same planet after all.'*"

John Gottman who co-authored a book with Nan Silver called "*The Seven Principles for Making Marriage Work*" continued by saying,
"*Happy marriages are based on a deep friendship. By this I mean a mutual respect for and enjoyment of each other's company. These couples tend to know each other intimately—they are well versed in each other's likes, dislikes, personality quirks, hopes, and dreams. They have an abiding regard for each other and express this fondness not just in the big ways but in little ways day in and day out. . . . Friendship fuels the flames of romance because it offers the best protection against feeling adversarial toward your spouse.*"

JESUS' FRIENDSHIPS

- The Trinity is a community of friendship.
- On earth, Jesus was friendly toward all but only friends with a few.
- Jesus' friends failed him and his true friends repented so the friendship could continue.
- We learn to befriend our spouse through our friendship with Jesus, who says in John 15:15-17, "I have called you friends...love one another."

3 KINDS of MARRIAGES

1. Back-to-Back
2. Shoulder-to-Shoulder
3. Face-to-Face

Marriage is about friendship (Real Marriage). {

FRUITFUL {F}

Genesis 1:28: "Be fruitful..."

Proverbs 18:24: "A man who has friends must himself be friendly."

Proverbs 20:18: "Plans are established by counsel; by wise guidance wage war."

Proverbs 24:5-6: "A wise man is strong, yes, a man of knowledge increases strength; for by wise counsel you will wage your own war, and in a multitude of counselors there is safety."

Proverbs 13:20: "He who walks with wise men will be wise, but the companion of fools will be destroyed."

QUESTION: What ministry to your family and other people has God set before you?

_____

_____

_____

> Wives overwhelmingly (70%) say sexual satisfaction is most impacted by the quality of their FRIENDSHIP with their spouse (Real Marriage).

{R} RECIPROCAL

Galatians 5:22: "The fruit of the Spirit is love."

Romans 5:5: "...The love of God has been poured out in our hearts by the Holy Spirit who was given to us."

1 Corinthians 13:4-7: "Love suffers long and is kind; love does not envy; love does not parade itself, is not puffed up; does not behave rudely, does not seek its own, is not provoked, thinks no evil; does not rejoice in iniquity, but rejoices in the truth; bears all things, believes all things, hopes all things, endures all things."

QUESTION: How can you be a better friend to your spouse, especially in the little acts of considerate love?

_____

_____

_____

{I} INTIMATE

Proverbs 18:24: "A man who has friends must himself be friendly, but there is a friend who sticks closer than a brother."

 Women: Cultivate friendships through shared communication.

 Men: Cultivate friendship through shared activity.

QUESTION: In what ways have I been a good friend? In what ways have I been a bad friend?

_____

_____

_____

ENJOYABLE

Ecclesiastes 9:7-9 : "Go, eat your bread with joy, and drink your wine with a merry heart; for God has already accepted your works. Let your garments always be white, and let your head lack no oil. Live joyfully with the wife whom you love all the days of your vain life which He has given you under the sun, all your days of vanity; for that is your portion in life, and in the labor which you perform under the sun." — Enjoy Life

— Be fun

QUESTION: What are your favorite memories together in the past, present, and possibly future?

_____

_____

_____

Gen 1:31 - Not good for man to be alone,

> Husbands and wives who want their marriages to be enduring and endearing must be friends (Real Marriage). {

NEEDED

Genesis 2:18: And the Lord God said, "It is not good that man should be alone; I will make him a helper comparable to him."

QUESTION: Fill in the blank: 'I need you because _____'.

> Marital friendship requires both the husband and wife truly investing in what it takes to be a good friend (Real Marriage). {

> Marriage is a journey between lovers & friends, but becomes a business partnership if we don't work on the friendship (Real Marriage).

{D} DEVOTED

Philippians 2:3-4: "In lowliness of mind . . . esteem others better than [your]self. Let each of you look out not only for his own interests, but also for the interests of others."

Romans 12:15: "Rejoice with those who rejoice, and weep with those who weep."

Proverbs 17:17: "A friend loves at all times, and a brother is born for adversity."

— The most important day is the last day.

QUESTION: How have you succeeded and failed at being a devoted friend?

_____

_____

_____

{S} SANCTIFYING

better or bitter

Ecclesiastes 4:9-10: "Two are better than one, because they have a good reward for their labor. For if they fall, one will lift up his companion. But woe to him who is alone when he falls, for he has no one to help him up."

Proverbs 27:6: "Faithful are the wounds of a friend, but the kisses of an enemy are deceitful."

Proverbs 27:9: "Ointment and perfume delight the heart, and the sweetness of a man's friend gives delight by hearty (which means to be honest) counsel."

— We see our sin & grow to be more like Jesus.

QUESTION: How is God using you to make one another more holy?

_____

_____

_____

WHAT NOW?

What are 1 to 2 practical things that you plan to do as a result of the teaching in this session?

1. _____

_____

_____

_____

2. _____

_____

_____

_____

your NOTES

TAKING out the TRASH

3

Confess your trespasses to one another, and pray for one another. **James 5:16**

BIG IDEA!

Every home accumulates trash, so we must take it out often. Failure to do so stinks up the entire home. Sin is like trash, and every home has it too. Repentance and forgiveness are how a couple takes out their trash.

If you are married, you will have conflict. You cannot avoid it because marriage is an unconditional commitment to an imperfect person.

$$[\ 1 \text{ sinner} + 1 \text{ sinner} \neq 0 \text{ conflict}\ ]$$

You *will* sin against your spouse, and your spouse *will* sin against you. Couples who claim to never fight are either lying or living completely passionless, independent, parallel lives, so emotionally distant that hurting each other is virtually impossible. You will fight. The question is, will you fight well to the glory of God and the good of your marriage?

HOW *NOT* TO FIGHT

Dr. John Gottman, among the world's most renowned marriage experts, has proven able to predict marriages that will end in divorce at a 91% rate. Using the apocalyptic language of the Bible, he lists four horsemen of marital death. Each relates to a marital fight, often beginning with a "harsh startup".

Horseman #1: Criticism that attacks the *person* not the *problem*. *always/never*

Horseman #2: Contempt that is rooted in disgust. *– feel ashamed*

Horseman #3: Defensiveness where the guilty person refuses to repent. *won't apologize*

Horseman #4: Stonewalling where one person shuts down or walks away.
(85% of the time it is the man)

> If you never fight, you probably aren't having heartfelt conversations that often lead to disagreement (Real Marriage).

– Take one to forgive, one to repent, and 2 to reconcile

HOW TO FIGHT TO THE GLORY of GOD
& GOOD OF YOUR MARRIAGE:

#1. UNDERSTAND SIN
Recognize Sin – violation of Word of God

- Sin of Commission
- Sin of Omission
- Sin of Thought
- Sin of Word
- Sin of Deed
- Sin of Motive

not personality
culture
Difference b/t sin & mistake

#2. PRACTICE REPENTANCE
Good Christians make good wives & husbands.

- Conviction
1 • Confession *– agree w/God*
2 • Contrition *– feel weight of sin*
3 • Change *– Do they want to change*

Luther – "All of a Christian's Life is one of repentance.

Js. 5:16

TAKING OUT THE TRASH **19**

Not getting caught, but coming clean.

> Couples who claim to never fight are either lying or living completely passionless, independent, parallel lives
> (Real Marriage).

Not worldly sorrow.

#3. PRACTICE FORGIVENESS & FIGHT BITTERNESS

Ephesians 4:25-32: "Putting away lying, 'Let each one of you speak truth with his neighbor,' for we are members of one another. 'Be angry, and do not sin': do not let the sun go down on your wrath, nor give place to the devil. Let him who stole steal no longer, but rather let him labor, working with his hands what is good, that he may have something to give him who has need. Let no corrupt word proceed out of your mouth, but what is good for necessary edification, that it may impart grace to the hearers. And do not grieve the Holy Spirit of God, by whom you were sealed for the day of redemption. Let all bitterness, wrath, anger, clamor, and evil speaking be put away from you, with all malice. And be kind to one another, tenderhearted, forgiving one another, even as God in Christ forgave you."

The only thing more powerful than sin is Jesus.

1. **Forgiveness** is not denying, approving, or diminishing sin that is committed against us. *Don't lie or conceal.*

The enemy is your enemy

2. **Forgiveness** is not naivety.

3. **Forgiveness** is not enabling sin.

Deal w/ things quickly

4. **Forgiveness** is not waiting for someone to acknowledge sin, apologize, and repent.

5. **Forgiveness** is not forgetting about sin committed against us.

6. **Forgiveness** is not dying emotionally and no longer feeling the pain of the transgression.

7. **Forgiveness** is not a one-time event.

8. **Forgiveness** is not reconciliation.

9. **Forgiveness** is not neglecting justice.

> We do not forgive our spouses because they are good or deserving, but rather because God is good and deserving
> (Real Marriage).

#4. AGREE TO GROUND RULES BEFORE THE FIGHT

1. Has your spouse committed a sin or simply made a mistake?

2. How will you deal with the conflict and avoid fight, flight, or fright?

3. Are either of you affected by a substance? If so, wait to talk.

4. How can you pray before, during, and after the fight?

5. Are you using a fight as a lightning rod or release valve?

6. If you cannot agree, should you let it go or get a pastor/counselor involved?

QUESTION: What do you need to repent of to your spouse, and what do you need to forgive your spouse for?

_____

_____

_____

As an act of worship, we must respond to our sinful spouses as
God has responded to our sin — with forgiveness
(Real Marriage).

WHAT NOW?

What are 1 to 2 practical things that you plan to do as a result of the teaching in this session?

1._____
_____
_____
_____

2._____
_____
_____
_____

SEX:GOD, GROSS, or GIFT?

They were both naked, the man and his wife, and were not ashamed. **Genesis 2:25**

BIG IDEA!

Most of the time, a couple enters into a marriage with different views of sex. And, even if they agree, rarely do they both agree with the Bible. How we are raised, teaching we have had (or not had), and experiences we have accumulated all combine to shape our view of sex. Three basic views are most common, sex as *god*, sex as *gross*, and sex as a *gift*.

1) God
2) gross
3) gift

SEX before SIN

Genesis 2:18-25: "And the Lord God said, 'It is not good that man should be alone; I will make him a helper comparable to him.' Out of the ground the Lord God formed every beast of the field and every bird of the air, and brought them to Adam to see what he would call them. And whatever Adam called each living creature, that was its name. So Adam gave names to all cattle, to the birds of the air, and to every beast of the field. But for Adam there was not found a helper comparable to him. And the Lord God caused a deep sleep to fall on Adam, and he slept; and He took one of his ribs, and closed up the flesh in its place. Then the rib which the Lord God had taken from man He made into a woman, and He brought her to the man. And Adam said: 'This is now bone of my bones and flesh of my flesh; she shall be called woman, because she was taken out of man.' Therefore a man shall leave his father and mother and be joined to his wife, and they shall become one flesh. And they were both naked, the man and his wife, and were not ashamed."

from side

"I love Jesus & I have a job"

WHAT WE SEE IN THIS TEXT:

1. *God made us male and female with equal dignity and differing roles.*

2. *Love is more like a song than a math equation.*
   Don't try to understand her.

3. *Marriage is for one man and one woman by God's design.*

4. *God created our bodies and sexual pleasure "very good."*
   A gift of God

5. *All sex outside of marriage is a sin.*

6. *Sex is to be without shame.*

✱7. *Your standard of beauty is your spouse.*   *You're into your spouse.*

> Your biggest sex organ is your brain. Thinking rightly about sex is essential to your enjoyment of sex (Real Marriage).

> A couple with a free and frequent sex life is bonded together as one, physically and chemically by God's design (Real Marriage).

THREE WAYS TO VIEW SEX:

SEX AS GOD: ~~Idolator~~ *sex is act of worship.*

Romans 12:1: "Present your bodies a living sacrifice."

1 Corinthians 10:7-8: "Do not become idolaters as some of them. As it is written, 'The people sat down to eat and drink, and rose up to play.' Nor let us commit sexual immorality, as some of them did."

Romans 1:18-19, 23-27: "For the wrath of God is revealed from heaven against all ungodliness and unrighteousness of men, who suppress the truth in unrighteousness, because what may be known of God is manifest in them, for God has shown it to them... made like corruptible man—and birds and four-footed animals and creeping things. Therefore God also gave them up to uncleanness, in the lusts of their hearts, to dishonor their bodies among themselves, who exchanged the truth of God for the lie, and worshiped and served the creature rather than the Creator, who is blessed forever. Amen. For this reason God gave them up to vile passions. For even their women exchanged the natural use for what is against nature. Likewise also the men, leaving the natural use of the woman, burned in their lust for one another, men with men committing what is shameful, and receiving in themselves the penalty of their error which was due."

[handwritten left margin: You know you're a pagan idolator when you are a pervert.]

> } Honesty, repentance, obedience to God, praying together against fear and for freedom—all lead to healthy intimacy
> (Real Marriage).

In *Real Marriage* we write,
"Annual pornography revenues are more than $90 billion worldwide. In the United States, pornography revenues were $13 billion in 2006, more than all combined revenues of professional football, baseball, and basketball franchises or the combined revenues of ABC, CBS, and NBC ($6.2 billion). Porn sites account for 12 percent of all Internet sites. Every day 2.5 million pornographic emails are sent. A staggering 90 percent of children between the ages of eight and sixteen have viewed pornography on the Internet, in most cases unintentionally. The average age of first Internet exposure to pornography is eleven years old. The largest consumer category of Internet pornography is twelve to seventeen-year-old boys. Youth with significant exposure to sexuality in the media were shown to be considerably more likely to have had intercourse at ages fourteen to sixteen."

> } Human orgasm affects the same parts of the brain that heroin and cocaine do (Real Marriage).

SEX AS GROSS: Reaction

1. Unbiblical Greek thinking. Dualistic
2. Errors in Church history. Only for pro-creation
3. Modern day religious prudery.
4. Those who have sinned sexually and/or been sinned against sexually.

SEX AS A GIFT:

1. **Pleasure** (Song of Songs)
2. **Children** (Genesis 1:28)
3. **Knowledge** (Genesis 4:1)
4. **Protection** (1 Corinthians 7:2-5) safeguard
5. **Comfort** (2 Samuel 12:24) Part of friendship
6. **Oneness** (Genesis 2:24)
   One Life / One-Woman Man

Dr. Stephen Arterburn's New Life Ministries says,
"Sexual pleasure is one of the most intense human experiences. Physically speaking, when a man or woman reaches sexual excitement, nerve endings release a chemical into the brain called 'opioid.' 'Opioid' means opium-like and is a good description of the power of this chemical. Apart from a heroin-induced experience, nothing is more physically pleasurable than sex. This is a wonderful thing in a committed marriage relationship, because it helps to bond two people together and bring joy to living together and building a relationship."

QUESTION: Are there any specific areas of your life where you
need to forgive your spouse? Anything you need to
let go of?

_____

_____

_____

WHAT NOW?

What are 1 to 2 practical things that you plan to do as a result of the teaching in this session?

1._____

_____

_____

_____

2._____

_____

_____

_____

SELFISH LOVERS & SERVANT LOVERS

5

Whoever desires to become great among you shall be your servant. **Mark 10:43**

BIG IDEA!

The Bible often commends people for having the attitude of a servant. Many of the apostles open their letters in the Bible declaring themselves to be servants. Jesus often referred to himself while on the earth as a servant, and this concept is very important for us to apply to our marriage so that we can be servant lovers instead of selfish lovers.

<u>Selfishness</u>
pride

~ Repackaged as self-esteem

Proverbs 8:13 - God hates pride
16:5 .
16:18

~ Holy Spirit clothe me in humility,
"God gives grace to the humble"
Jesus

←————————————————→
selfish   10
                            servant

~ How do we become great?
MK 10:43ff

YOU ARE SELFISH

1. The World
2. The Flesh
3. The Devil

Pride is the default mode of the human heart (Real Marriage). {

SELFISHNESS OFTEN MANIFESTS
in the "LITTLE THINGS"

- Song of Songs 2:15 speaks of "the little foxes that spoil the vines."
- Selfish + Selfish = Brutal Marriage.
- Selfish + Servant = Abusive Marriage.
- Servant + Servant = Godly Marriage.

little things hurt a marriage

— What is it for you?

Once we marry, we expect our spouses to serve us humbly, only
to find they were expecting the same thing (Real Marriage). {

— Do you consider your spouse need above own?

HUMILITY, LOVE, & SERVICE

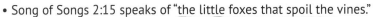

humility

Philippians 2:3-8: "In lowliness of mind let each esteem others better than himself. Let each of you look out not only for his own interests, but also for the interests of others. Let this mind be in you which was also in Christ Jesus, who, being in the form of God, did not consider it robbery to be equal with God, but made Himself of no reputation, taking the form of a bondservant, and coming in the likeness of men. And being found in appearance as a man, He humbled Himself."

Can't love and use.
— Do you receive instruction?
— Do you encourage or criticize?
— Do you serve & are willing to be served?
— Do you continually ask HS to make you humble?

SERVANT LOVERS

Christian couples should have sex (handwritten)

1 Corinthians 7:3-5: "Let the husband render to his wife the affection due her, and likewise also the wife to her husband. The wife does not have authority over her own body, but the husband does. And likewise the husband does not have authority over his own body, but the wife does. Do not deprive one another except with consent for a time, that you may give yourselves to fasting and prayer; and come together again so that Satan does not tempt you because of your lack of self-control." *Offense / Defense* (handwritten)

meet each other's needs (handwritten left margin)

> We must willfully, earnestly, and continually humble ourselves (Real Marriage).

— Serve Spouse (handwritten)

SEXUAL FREQUENCY

In *Real Marriage* we write,
"*The younger a couple, as a general rule, the more sex they have. One study reported that couples under the age of twenty-four had a mean frequency of sex about 132 times a year, which is about 11 times per month, or once every 2–3 days. Another more recent report said, 'Married people under thirty have sex about 111 times a year' which is about 9 times a month, or 2–3 times a week. The report goes on to say, 'Married men and women, on average, have sex with their spouse 58 times a year, a little more than once a week.' The number of what is average sexual frequency for a married couple is greatly affected downward by the fact 'about 15 percent of married couples have not had sex with their spouse in the last six months to one year.' According to a 2003 Newsweek study, between 15 and 20 percent of couples are living in a sexless marriage—meaning they have sex no more than ten times a year.*"

WAYS WE ARE SELFISH LOVERS:

1. *Rarely have sex.*
2. *Too little time and too little effort.*
3. *Only have sex when you both feel like it at the same time.*
4. *We rarely initiate.*
5. *Let ourselves go – become undesirable.*
6. *Sexual sabotage.*
7. *Make our spouses earn sex.*
8. *Sharing our bed with children and pets.*
9. *Separate beds or rooms.*

BEING VISUALLY GENEROUS

Roughly 25% of women and nearly 100% of men are "visual."

Song of Songs 6:13-7:13 (NIV) : "Why would you gaze on the Shulammite as on the dance of Mahanaim? How beautiful your sandaled feet, O prince's daughter! Your graceful legs are like jewels, the work of a craftsman's hands. Your navel is a rounded goblet that never lacks blended wine. Your waist is a mound of wheat encircled by lilies. Your breasts are like two fawns, twins of a gazelle. Your neck is like an ivory tower. Your eyes are the pools of Heshbon by the gate of Bath Rabbim. Your nose is like the tower of Lebanon looking toward Damascus. Your head crowns you like Mount Carmel. Your hair is like royal tapestry; the king is held captive by its tresses. How beautiful you are and how pleasing, O love, with your delights! Your stature is like that of the palm, and your breasts like clusters of fruit. I said, 'I will climb the palm tree; I will take hold of its fruit.' May your breasts be like the clusters of the vine, the fragrance of your breath like apples, and your mouth like the best wine. May the wine go straight to my lover, flowing gently over lips and teeth. I belong to my lover, and his desire is for me. Come, my lover, let us go to the countryside, let us spend the night in the villages. Let us go early to the vineyards to see if the vines have budded, if their blossoms have opened, and if the pomegranates are in bloom — there I will give you my love. The mandrakes send out their fragrance, and at our door is every delicacy, both new and old, that I have stored up for you, my lover. How beautiful your sandaled feet, O prince's daughter!"

QUESTION: In regards to sex, are you more prone toward
being selfish or a servant?

_____

_____

_____

WHAT NOW?

What are 1 to 2 practical things that you plan to do as a result of the teaching in this session?

1._____

_____

_____

_____

2._____

_____

_____

_____

EVERYONE
HAS A ROLE IN
LIFE
WE GO TO THE HARD PLACES.
fh
food for the hungry
Artist Program
www.fh.org

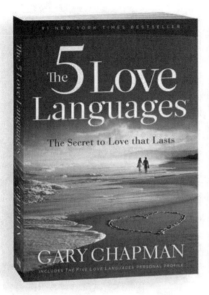
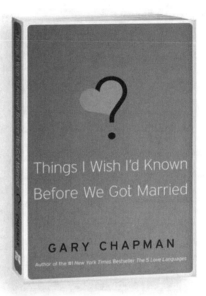

CAN WE ___ IF WE'RE MARRIED?

This and more at pastormark.tv

RESURGENCE
OVER TWO MILLION LEADERS SERVED EVERY YEAR

Our mission is to serve leaders, and to help equip you for your God-given mission. How can we serve you?

EACH YEAR, MILLIONS OF LEADERS TRUST RESURGENCE FOR:

TIMELY ARTICLES

As the highest visited Christian leadership blog, we feature articles from prominent Evangelical leaders addressing the challenges of ministry in a post-Christian society.

BOOKS

Re:lit has published dozens of books to equip leaders on theology and practical ministry.

EVENTS

Resurgence conferences bring together some of the world's top speakers and preachers to transform hearts and minds for ministry action.

TEACHING

Podcast and vodcasts feature select talks and lectures from Resurgence events.

TRAINING

Re:train is a master's-level theology center with some of the best professors in the world, as well as practical training for day-to-day ministry from some of the most well-known and respected pastors today.

 For more information visit:
www.theresurgence.com

APPENDIX

"GETTING TO KNOW YOUR SPOUSE" QUESTIONNAIRE

The following questions are many of the same ones we use for the premarital counseling at our church as an assignment for those wanting to be married. In offering them we are not expecting anyone to go through them all, or worse still, to use them like an interrogation. Instead, over the course of many conversations, it might be interesting to comb through the questions and ask your spouse some of the more curious ones you stumble across and then listen respectfully to see what you can learn.

SPIRITUAL BACKGROUND

1. What is the gospel?

2. Who is Jesus?

3. Do you consider yourself a Christian? Why?

4. What role do you want to see Jesus playing in your marriage?

5. What kind of religious upbringing did you have?

6. How did your parents influence your beliefs of God?

7. List ways that your family exhibited a faith or belief in God (prayer before meals, reading the Bible together, etc.).

8. Have you been baptized? When?

9. How do you practice spiritual disciplines (prayer, Bible reading, attend church, etc.)?

10. What is sin?

11. What sins do you struggle with most frequently?

12. How pleased are you with your spiritual life together, including praying, attending church, being in a Bible study small group, and serving God?

13. How would you describe your personal journey as a Christian?

14. How strong do you think your faith is?

15. What have been the highlights of your relationship with Christ and of your church or ministry involvement?

16. What are the main ways you've seen God active in and through you?

17. What are some special times when you have seen God provide for you?

18. When were some times when you felt that you were not walking with God very closely? Why do you think that happened?

19. What are some areas in which you want to see God work in your life?

AUTHORITY FIGURES

1. As you look at your past, how have you traditionally responded to authority (for example, parents, employers, teachers, coaches, pastors)?

2. How have you responded to Christ's authority in your life?

3. How do you think the way you respond to authority will affect your relationship with your future spouse?

4. As a wife, do you respect your husband, enable him, or disrespect him?

5. As a husband, do you lead lovingly or abdicate leadership to your wife?

FAMILY HISTORY

1. Were your parents divorced? If so, did they remarry? If so, which parent got custody of you?

2. How would you describe your parents' marriage?

3. Choose three to five adjectives to describe your relationship with your father and why you chose them.

4. Choose three to five adjectives to describe your relationship with your mother and why you chose them.

5. In what ways are you like your parents?

6. In what ways are you different?

7. In what ways do you want to emulate your parents' relationship?

8. What are the ways you do not want to emulate their relationship?

9. Are there any unresolved issues between you and your parents? Explain.

10. How well do you think you have left your parents to unite as a new family with your spouse?

11. What were your parents' expectations of you at school, work, or in sports?

12. What kind of prejudices do your parents have, if any?

13. What traditions do you want to pass on to your family? What traditions do you not want to pass on to your family?

14. In what ways did you rebel against your parents?

15. What kind of neighborhood did you grow up in?

16. Who worked in your family (mom, dad, both)?

17. Would you describe your family as poor, middle class, fairly affluent, wealthy, rich?

18. Who disciplined you? Did your parents agree on discipline?

19. Was your home open (frequent visitors and activities), closed (more structured meals, etc., and less visitors coming and going) or even random (no set schedule, people coming and going, even dangerous lack of oversight)?

20. How expressive was your family in word and deed?

21. How did your family address sensitive subjects?

22. Who made the rules? Who enforced the rules?

23. What was the standard of living in your home?

24. How did your family view finances and debt?

25. Who controlled the money?

26. Who was in charge? Who made the decisions?

27. How did your father divide his time between work and family? Was it balanced?

28. How did you learn about sex?

29. How did your family view work?

30. How did your family view recreation?

31. How did your family view education?

32. How did your family view politics?

33. How did your parents divide household responsibilities?

34. What values held priority in your home?

35. What things did your family do for recreation?

36. What did your family do for vacations?

37. How did your family handle holidays?

38. How did your family handle birthdays?

39. What was it like to be sick in your home?

40. How did your family manage the television, phone, computer, and other technology?

41. Did your family eat meals together?

42. What were the bedtime routines in your home?

43. How did your family relate to, for example, grandparents, aunts, uncles, cousins?

44. What were the highlights of your family?

45. What were the lowlights of your family?

46. How much privacy were you given at home?

47. How much freedom and independence were you given?

48. How many times did you move growing up?

49. Was your family public or private about their struggles and frustrations?

OTHER RELATIONSHIPS

1. How did you choose your friends?

2. How long do most of your friendships last? Why?

3. If you have had any long, enduring friendships, what has kept them going? If not, what are some reasons?

4. Have you been damaged by any of these relationships? How? If yes, how can God help you reverse the damage?

5. Is there any history of violence or sexual abuse in your past relationships?

6. Have you been previously married or engaged? If so, please explain.

7. Have you ever had a homosexual or bisexual experience? If so, please explain.

WORK & CAREER

1. On a scale of 1 to 10 (1 being bad, 10 being good) how would you rate your work ethic? Why?

2. How many jobs have you held in the past five years? Why did you change jobs (if you did)?

3. At what age did you begin working? Why?

FINANCES

1. How much financial debt do you have, including credit cards, car payments, school loans, mortgage? Please list all debt.

2. What are your attitudes and beliefs regarding money?

3. Have you ever declared bankruptcy?

4. Do you believe your giving to God is adequate?

5. Do you believe you need to grow in issues related to stewarding your finances? What should you do to accomplish that?

COUPLE RELATIONSHIP

1. Have you been engaged before? Explain.

2. What do your parents, other family members, and friends think of your relationship? Does anyone disapprove?

3. What are your character strengths? Weaknesses?

4. As a couple, what are the strengths of your relationship?

5. As a couple, in what areas do you need to grow in your relationship?

6. How well do you make decisions together? How could you improve this area of your marriage?

7. What has been most difficult about marriage? Why? How could your spouse help you?

8. What are five reasons you married your spouse?

9. Are there any areas of concerns you have about him or her? (Some areas of concern might be lack of common interests, frequent arguments, or anger concerns.)

10. Has he or she ever pushed you, grabbed you, yelled at you, threatened you, or demonstrated other abusive behaviors?

11. Have you discussed having children? How many? When? Will she work after you have children?

12. What attracted you to each other?

13. What are some of the favorite things you've done together?

OTHER PERSONAL QUESTIONS

1. Have you ever been arrested for a crime? When?

2. Have you ever used any drugs? When was the last time?

3. Have you ever used alcohol to excess? Explain.

4. Have you ever experienced any compulsions or addictions (food, drugs, alcohol)?

5. Is there any history of chemical dependency or addiction in your family?

6. Have you ever experienced abuse (sexual, mental, emotional, physical)? Explain.

7. Have you experienced an eating disorder?

8. How is your current physical and mental health?

9. Have you ever been clinically diagnosed with a mental illness, including dissociative, depressed, borderline, bipolar I or II, panic or anxiety disorder?

10. Is there any history of mental illness in your family?

11. Have you received professional counseling (psychologist, psychiatrist) or lay counseling through a church? When and for what reasons?

12. Have you ever experienced problems with anger? Describe.

13. Have you ever attempted suicide or do you have suicidal thoughts? Explain.

SEXUAL HISTORY (Please explain your answers)

1. What is your complete sexual history in addition to your spouse?

2. *Women:* Have you been pregnant before? Do you have any children from a previous relationship?

3. *Men:* Have you gotten anyone pregnant before? Do you have any children from a previous relationship?

4. Have you ever been diagnosed with a sexually transmitted disease?

5. If you have been sexually active in the past, have you been tested for STDs?

6. Is there any history of violence or sexual abuse in your past or current relationship?

7. Have you had any sexual contact with anyone else during your current relationship?

8. Have you ever experienced a same-sex attraction?

9. What is your experience with pornography? Explain: when, for how long, and the last time you viewed it.

10. Are you currently using pornography at all? Explain.

11. Have you experienced ongoing guilt and shame from past sexual sins?

12. Have you been completely honest in answering these questions? Are you withholding anything or keeping something secret? It might seem too hard to tell this information, but lying to your spouse only delays the pain and keeps sin between you, causing division.

APPENDIX

DATE NIGHT TIPS

DATE NIGHT TIP 1
Parents: if you cannot afford a sitter, is there a way to set up a rotation with other families to take turns each week watching kids for date night? If you have four families, you can get a date night three times a month.

DATE NIGHT TIP 2
Husbands: when is your date night? Your wife needs it. You do too. We've enjoyed Friday date nights for about twenty years.

DATE NIGHT TIP 3
Husbands: don't waste every date night at a movie where you can't talk. Use the time to visit with your wife, draw her out, and study her as you do the Bible.

DATE NIGHT TIP 4
Plan out your date nights. Ask your spouse in advance what sounds good, ask their options, make a plan, and they'll be thankful.

DATE NIGHT TIP 5
Avoid date night killers: having no plan, selfishness, laziness, letting technology keep interrupting, and doing the same old predictable thing.

DATE NIGHT TIP 6
Time with other couples now and then is okay, but if most date nights involve other people, there is likely an intimacy disconnect in the marriage.

DATE NIGHT TIP 7
Dads: moms who stay home all day with kids need to get dressed up, be taken out, and have some adult conversation with their husband.

DATE NIGHT TIP 8
Husbands: what can you do to find some creative ways to make date night fun and endearing even on a tight budget?

DATE NIGHT TIP 9
Husbands: what can you start doing days or hours before date night to build the expectation of connection with your wife? Flowers, cards, calls, texts?

DATE NIGHT TIP 10
When life gets crazy, for example, the kids are sick, find a way to sneak in a bit of a date night at home, such as a soak in the tub together or a glass of wine after the kids go to sleep.

DATE NIGHT TIP 11
Sometimes sending the kids out to someone's house and having a date night at home can be cheap and fun if planned right.

DATE NIGHT TIP 12
Men: you don't pursue a woman to marry her and then stop pursuing her. You pursue a woman to marry her and pursue her with more passion and creativity than ever. How's it going, husbands?

DATE NIGHT TIP 13
Men: you don't need to understand women. You will be doing better than most to understand one woman. Date nights are to ask inviting questions, listen, and learn about her. It's also a night to open up and let her do the same. Engage in conversation.

DATE NIGHT TIP 14
Men: if you don't date your wife, someone else may eventually volunteer for the job.

DATE NIGHT TIP 15
Ladies: sometimes it's a great gift to go into your husband's world for a date night by doing something like putting on a jersey, going to a game, and eating a hot dog. His love language may just be hot dog.

DATE NIGHT TIP 16
Men: here are some date night tips just for you: find a shirt with buttons, try two eyebrows instead of one for a change, find a breath mint or twenty, show up with a gift, don't ogle other women, and go to a restaurant that does not have a spork.

DATE NIGHT TIP 17
Sometimes the best date night is date breakfast, date lunch, or surprise pick-up-your-spouse-from-work for an hour at a hotel.

DATE NIGHT TIP 18
For some they are "bored" games, but if your spouse likes board games, a fun date night is to find a nice spot to be (like the beach) with a beverage of choice and time to play and chat.

DATE NIGHT TIP 19
Sometimes takeout is fun and a drive to somewhere more private to turn it into a picnic or adventure.

DATE NIGHT TIP 20
A nice, relaxing candlelight massage is always a good date night, especially if your spouse is high touch.

DATE NIGHT TIP 21
Every once in a while, you just have to have a redneck date night and go bowling, play pool, or throw darts.

DATE NIGHT TIP 22
Plan in advance for some big events like concerts, comedians, plays, or a cirque show. Who is coming to town? What would be fun?

DATE NIGHT TIP 23

Men: take your wife shopping. Yes, shopping at a place that does not also sell carburetors or fishing supplies. Patiently help her pick things out, watch her try them on, flatter her with comments, and spend some money.

DATE NIGHT TIP 24

Sometimes it's fun to go on an old memorable date again, or retrace a first date, relive the memory, and remember what God has done since then.

DATE NIGHT TIP 25

A few times a year, a couple needs an overnight date. Even if it's a night away with a discount room from Priceline, dinner out, and time to chill.

DATE NIGHT TIP 26

If you have no idea what to talk about on date night, take turns picking a book, each read a chapter a week, and discuss what you learned on date night to kickstart conversation.

DATE NIGHT TIP 27

Husbands, have you ever asked your wife what things she's always wanted to do but never told you? You could plan some epic date nights from that list.

DATE NIGHT TIP 28

It's always a good idea to take a camera on date night, snap some photos, and revisit them to have a laugh and celebrate the times you've enjoyed.

DATE NIGHT TIP 29

If money is tight for date nights, ask family and friends for gift cards to places you like (as birthday and holiday presents). Then after you use them, send them a thank you so they know what a blessing it was.

APPENDIX III

DIVORCE & REMARRIAGE

Divorce and remarriage are such complicated issues that there is no way we can do the subjects justice in anything short of a book devoted entirely to the topic. Our basic position is that while God loves the divorced person, God hates divorce[1] because of all the pain of sin that causes it to occur and results from it. This pain includes both spouses, their children, friends, extended family, and future generations who endure emotional, financial, and other consequences. For these reasons, divorcees also agree that they, too, hate divorce.

In an effort to be of some help, however, we will briefly answer some of the most common questions regarding divorce and remarriage. For anyone considering divorce, you will need to meet with a godly pastor and possibly a Biblical counselor before any such decision is made.

What constitutes the legitimate ending of a marriage?

1. Death[2]
2. Adultery[3]
3. Non-Christian files for divorce and leaves[4]
4. Sexual immorality/porneia[5]
5. Treachery or treasonous betrayal[6]
6. Hardness of heart[7]

What should church leaders do if my Christian spouse insists on divorcing me?

Investigate grounds, possible discipline, with the goal of saving the marriage.

- He [Jesus] said to them, "Whoever divorces his wife and marries another commits adultery against her. And if a woman divorces her husband and marries another, she commits adultery." *(Mark 10:11–12)*

- The woman who has a husband is bound by the law to her husband as long as he lives. *(Romans 7:2–3)*

- Now to the married, I command, yet not I but the Lord: A wife is not to depart from her husband. But even if she does depart, let her remain unmarried or be reconciled to her husband. And a husband is not to divorce his wife. *(1 Corinthians 7:10–11)*

- Are you bound to a wife? Do not seek to be loosed. *(1 Corinthians 7:27)*

Does this mean people must endure abusive relationships?

No. In places like 1 Peter 3:7, the Bible commands men to love their wives and not be harsh with them. If there is abuse, the victim(s) must be separated from the abuser to a safe place. If the abuser does not get help and show complete change of mind and behavior, then divorce on grounds 5 and 6 above would be met for a possible divorce.

---

[1] *Mal. 2:16*
[2] *Rom. 7:2–4; 1 Cor. 7:39*
[3] *Deut. 22:22; Matt. 5:32*
[4] *1 Cor. 7:10–24*
[5] *Matt. 5:32; 19:9*
[6] *Mal. 2:14-16*
[7] *Matt. 19:8; Mark 10:5*

Am I required to take back my spouse after they have committed adultery?

No, in light of grounds 2 and 4 above. If someone does reconcile with an adulterating spouse, they are extending much grace, which by definition is not required but is noble.

Can I remarry if my spouse dies?

Yes.[8]

Can I remarry after a divorce that occurred because my spouse was an adulterer?

The parameters for remarriage are as follows:

- The innocent party of a divorce due to adultery may remarry but not the person guilty of adultery.

    Jesus replied, "'You shall not murder,' 'You shall not commit adultery.'"
    (Matt. 19:18)

    In the house His disciples also asked Him [Jesus] about the same matter. So He said to them, "Whoever divorces his wife and marries another commits adultery against her. And if a woman divorces her husband and marries another, she commits adultery."
    (Mark 10:10–12)

    Whoever divorces his wife and marries another commits adultery; and whoever marries her who is divorced from her husband commits adultery.
    (Luke 16:18)

- A believer is divorced by an unbeliever who leaves him or her.

    But if the unbeliever departs, let him depart; a brother or sister is not under bondage in such cases. But God has called us to peace. *(1 Cor. 7:15)*

- Lastly, if someone was divorced as a non-Christian and later became a Christian, it is possible for them to marry another Christian.

What if I divorced my spouse because of domestic violence, child abuse, or abandonment—can I remarry?

While you may be free to remarry, you first will require pastoral or professional help or both. You need to recover from your previous marriage and be careful not to enter into another unhealthy relationship.

In closing, these are very complicated issues. Any attempt to put a neat and tidy set of rules in place is invariably abused by sinful people who find ways to make their sin fit such grids. Therefore, God gives wisdom to the church leaders who, along with governmental laws, can help make these decisions. Ultimately, none of these kinds of questions can be answered for an individual case unless spiritual leaders are involved, getting both sides of the story, to carefully and prayerfully come to a wise decision. We have done this many times in our years of ministry together and rarely counsel someone to seek a divorce. We always work toward repentance and reconciliation while acknowledging that sometimes those things simply do not occur and we have to do the best with the situation we have.

---

[8] *Rom. 7:2–4; 1 Cor. 7:39*

APPENDIX IV

MARRIAGE TO AN UNBELIEVER

The Bible commands Christians not to marry non-Christians.[1]

But it can happen in a number of ways.

Sometimes Christians sin and marry non-Christians.

Christians believe they are marrying other Christians, but over time the believers discover their spouses never actually were Christians, or that they had turned their backs on God and decided not to live as Christians.

Two non-Christians marry, but one spouse converts while the other does not.

What the believing spouse is supposed to do in marriage with an unbelieving spouse can become complicated and painful. As a ministry couple, this scenario is a reality for some people we love very much. And although we cannot cover this subject in detail, we did want to give some counsel in an effort to encourage and serve those Christians who are married to non-Christians.

In the Bible, the places you will want to study most intently are 1 Peter 3:1–6 and 1 Corinthians 7:12–16. Also, the book of Esther is very helpful as it tells the story of a believing woman married to an unbelieving man and who conducted herself admirably.

Because it is God who saves, praying frequently for your spouse is key. This also will keep your heart from growing hard toward your spouse. A handful of godly friends of the same gender praying with you, and for you and your spouse, will be helpful.

You will likely need to be patient, especially if you are a believing woman married to an unbelieving man. All the studies we have read on this subject reveal the same thing—a believing man is more likely to see his unbelieving wife converted than a believing woman is to see her unbelieving husband converted.

You need to live your life as a Christian—going to church, reading your Bible, and growing in Christ. This needs to be done in a humble and considerate manner, but you cannot wait for your spouse to convert to live as a Christian. Your chief goal is to honor and glorify God. You should do this in an effort to see the conversion of your spouse and preservation of your marriage also. But if your spouse demands you sin against God or cease walking with God, then you cannot accommodate your spouse's demands, even if it tragically means the marriage will end as a result.

---

[1] *2 Cor. 6:14*

A few books may be of help. *Surviving a Spiritual Mismatch in Marriage* by Lee and Leslie Strobel (Grand Rapids, MI: Zondervan, 2002) tells the story of how a godly wife helped her atheist husband become a Christian and a pastor. *How Women Help Men Find God* by David Murrow (Nashville:Thomas Nelson, 2008) gives some very helpful practical advice from his extensive study of how men meet God and connect with church.

kindle fire

GIVEAWAY

Thank you for attending the Real Marriage Tour. At the end of the conference, we'll be giving away a **FREE Amazon Kindle Fire** preloaded with Pastor Mark Driscoll's sermon archive and e-books of Real Marriage, Doctrine, Religion Saves, and many more.

ENTERING IS EASY. ALL YOU HAVE TO DO IS:

- Like the Real Marriage Tour on Facebook at **www.facebook.com/rmtour**

- If you haven't already, sign up for the iPad 2 giveaway and share it with your friends. The more you share, the more chances you have to win!

- Upload photos from the conference onto the page or tag Real Marriage in your photos.

We'll select one winner at each event from photos that are uploaded at each stop on the tour.

- A friend doubles the joy & cuts the grief in half.
- 3 kinds of marriage:
  a. Back to Back
     enemies
  b. Shoulder to shoulder
     business partners / child-centered
  c. Face-to-face
- Reasons God made marriage:
  a. "Be Fruitful"
  b. "Be Reciprocal"
     - Take two
  c. "Be Intimate"